JOURNEY THROUGH A DESERT

BY K.C. KELLEY

AMICUS READERS ● AMICUS INK

amicus
readers

Amicus Readers and Amicus Ink are imprints of Amicus
P.O. Box 1329, Mankato, MN 56002
www.amicuspublishing.us

Names: Kelley, K. C., author.
Title: Journey through a desert / by K.C. Kelley.
Description: Mankato, MN : Amicus, [2018] I Series: Amazing adventures I
  Description based on print version record and CIP data provided by
  publisher; resource not viewed.
Identifiers: LCCN 2017022596 (print) I LCCN 2017031600 (ebook) I ISBN
  9781681513492 (pdf) I ISBN 9781681513133 (library binding : alk. paper) I
  ISBN 9781681522692 (pbk. : alk. paper)
Subjects: LCSH: Desert ecology--Juvenile literature. I Deserts--Juvenile
  literature. I Desert animals--Juvenile literature.
Classification: LCC QH541.5.D4 (ebook) I LCC QH541.5.D4 K45 2018 (print) I
  DDC 551.41/5--dc23
LC record available at https://lccn.loc.gov/2017022596

Editor: Marysa Storm/Megan Peterson
Designer: Patty Kelley
Photo Researcher/Producer: Shoreline Publishing Group LLC

Photo Credits:
Cover: Nadezhda1906/Dreamstime.com
Dreamstime.com: Euotech 9, Adogslifephoto 16T, Matthjis Kuijpers 16TB, Rinus Baak 16R;
iStock: Jearlwebb 3, Chalabala 4; Shutterstock: Mark Skalny 7, Nick Fox 12, Oleksandr Lysenko 15.

Printed in China.

HC 10 9 8 7 6 5 4 3 2 1
PB 10 9 8 7 6 5 4 3 2 1

Deserts are beautiful.
Let's visit one!

The sand is soft.
It's hard for
Joe to walk!

Deserts are hot.
Zoe drinks lots
of water!

Plants grow
in the desert.
Don't touch
the cactus!

Animals live here, too.
Logan sees a rabbit!

People live in
deserts, too.

Our trip is over.
Time to cool off!

DESERT ANIMALS

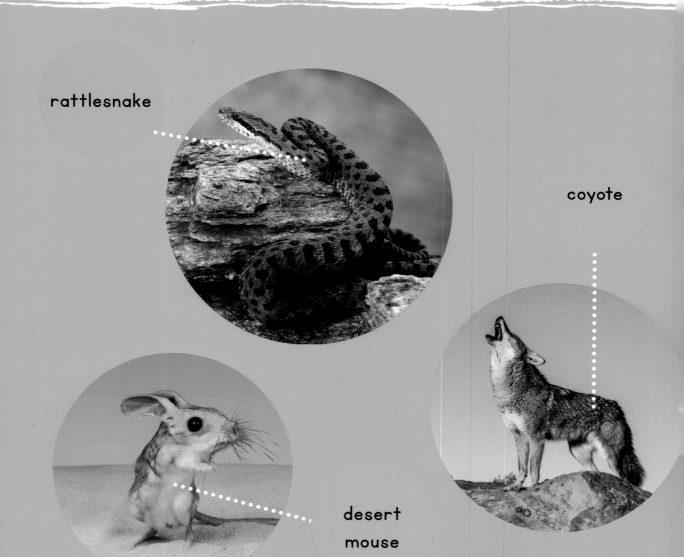

rattlesnake

coyote

desert
mouse